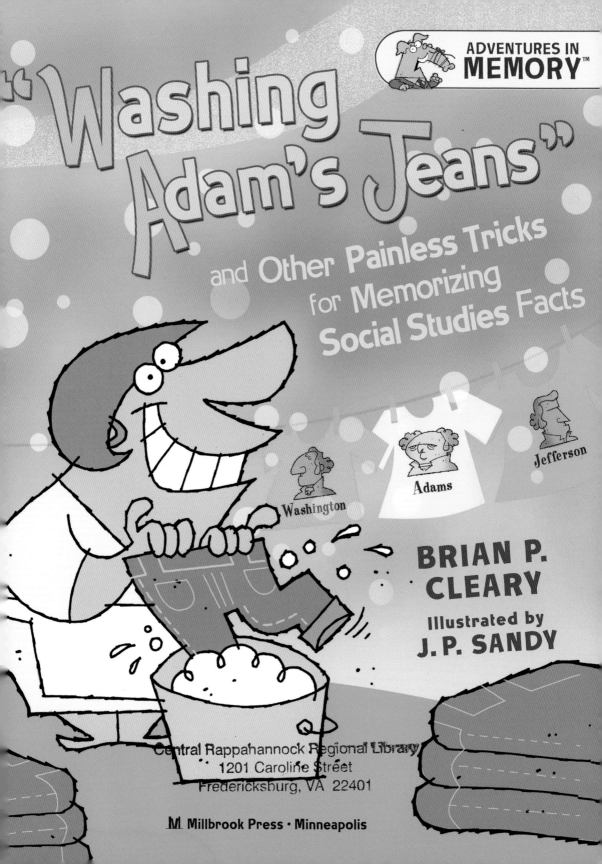

ADVENTURES IN
MEMORY™

"Washing
Adam's Jeans"

and Other Painless Tricks
for Memorizing
Social Studies Facts

Washington   Adams   Jefferson

BRIAN P.
CLEARY

Illustrated by
J. P. SANDY

M Millbrook Press · Minneapolis

To my daughter Emma
—B.P.C.

To Mom and Dad, Jim and Dianne Sandy
—J.P.S.

Millbrook Press
A division of Lerner Publishing Group, Inc.
241 First Avenue North
Minneapolis, MN 55401 U.S.A.

Website address: www.lernerbooks.com

Library of Congress Cataloging-in-Publication Data

Cleary, Brian P., 1959-
      "Washing Adam's jeans" and other painless tricks for memorizing social
   studies facts / by Brian P. Cleary ; illustrated by J. P. Sandy.
         p.   cm. — (Adventures in memory)
      Includes index.
      ISBN: 978-0-8225-7821-5 (lib. bdg. : alk. paper)
      1. Social sciences—Study and teaching. 2. Mnemonics. I. Sandy, J. P., ill. II. Title.
   H62.C54 2011
   300.71—dc22   2009014099

Manufactured in the United States of America
1 - DP - 7/15/10

INTRODUCTION 4
HOW THIS BOOK WILL HELP YOU MEMORIZE SOCIAL STUDIES FACTS

HISTORIC FIGURES of the WORLD 6

THE EXPLORATION STATION 6

FOUNDING of the UNITED STATES 14

HIP-HOP HISTORY: THE MAYFLOWER COMPACT 14
WE'RE HISTORY 16
WHO WROTE THE DECLARATION OF INDEPENDENCE? 18
THE THREE BRANCHES OF THE U.S. GOVERNMENT 19
KEY BATTLES OF THE AMERICAN REVOLUTION 20

THE PRESIDENTS of the UNITED STATES 22

THE FIRST 10 PRESIDENTS 22
PRESIDENTS 11 THROUGH 20 24
PRESIDENTS 21 THROUGH 30 26
PRESIDENTS 31 THROUGH 40 28
PRESIDENTS 41 THROUGH 44 30

THE CIVIL WAR 32

THE CONFEDERACY 32
THE UNION 34
THE EMANCIPATION PROCLAMATION 36
THE CIVIL WAR ENDS 37

HISTORIC FIGURES of the UNITED STATES 38

U.S. TRAILBLAZERS 38

ANSWER KEY 44

GLOSSARY 45

READ ON! 47

INDEX 48

HOW THIS BOOK WILL HELP YOU MEMORIZE SOCIAL STUDIES FACTS

Mnemonic
(pronounced *nih-MAH-nik*)

is a fancy word given to little tricks or devices that help us memorize important facts. Some of them rhyme, such as,

"Columbus sailed the ocean blue in fourteen hundred ninety-two."

Other memory aids build a word made up of the first letters of a list we're trying to memorize. **HOMES** is a trick for remembering the names of the five great lakes (**H**uron, **O**ntario, **M**ichigan, **E**rie, and **S**uperior). The word HOMES contains the first letter of the name of each lake.

Still other memory tools are more visual, meaning that a picture will help us to remember a fact, such as this one: A **Bactrian** camel has a back shaped like the letter **"B"** turned on its side. A **Dromedary** camel has a back shaped like the letter **"D"** turned on its side. So we know a Bactrian camel has two humps and a Dromedary camel has one.

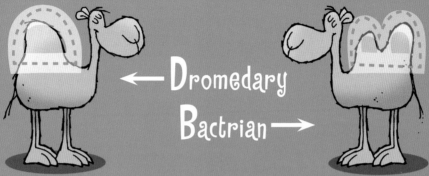

← Dromedary

Bactrian →

In this book, you'll find lots of fun ways to memorize social studies facts. But what I'm really hoping is that you'll develop your own tricks. Oftentimes the words, silly rhymes, or crazy sentences that you invent will be the most meaningful way for you to master social studies!

Here's an example of a way I came up with to remember the first ten presidents of the United States: **WASHING ADAM'S JE**ans, **MA MO**cked **A**unt **JACK**ie's **VA**luable **H**og, **TYLER**. This might help you remember: **WASHING**ton, **ADAMS**, **JE**fferson, **MA**dison, **MO**nroe, **A**dams, **JACK**son, **VA**n Buren, **H**arrison, and **TYLER**. But what if you're named Adam Jones and you have a hamster named Tyrone? Then you might find it memorable to say:

WASHING ADAM'S JEans, **MA MO**cked **ADAM J**ones's **VA**luable **HA**mster, **TY**rone. Sometimes, it's the absurd nature of what you've come up with that will help you to remember. They say **elephants never forget**. Well, now that you know about mnemonics, neither will you!

THE EXPLORATION STATION

Unscramble the captions to discover the names of different explorers. Each cartoon gives a clue to the explorer's identity. Find the answers on page 44.

I landed in what is now the Bahamas in 1492 and then sailed to Cuba and Hispaniola, an island that Haiti and the Dominican Republic share today.

Go Discover a NEW WORLD!

Help Tom Scour His Curb.

A Cool Prom

Best known by my three-word nickname, I'm a Viking explorer who colonized Greenland (which was not at all green and was quite icy).

In 1534 I discovered the mouth of the Saint Lawrence River in present-day Canada while I was trying to find a way west to the Pacific Ocean.

Acquire Car Jets

Raw Dance Skill

HIP-HOP HISTORY:
THE MAYFLOWER COMPACT

If you can memorize this rap, then you'll have all the important facts about the Mayflower Compact on the tip of your tongue.

EXTRA CREDIT
The pilgrims reached the New World in November 1620. Illness, poor food, and cold weather killed nearly half of the *Mayflower*'s passengers by spring 1621.

The Mayflower Compact
is kind of a pact
the settlers wrote up
to say how they'd act.

In this New World oasis,
it laid down the basis
for many famous documents
that his-tor-y traces.

'Cuz in this first contract,
the pilgrims agreed
their gov-ern-ment
had to be strong to succeed.

And so they'd be reminded
of those who designed it,
in 1620, they all wrote it
and signed it.

READ ON:
Learn more about the pilgrims in
*Why Did the Pilgrims Come to the
New World? And Other Questions
about the Plymouth Colony* by
Laura Hamilton Waxman.

WE'RE HISTORY

A Poem about the Declaration of Independence

Memorize this poem and you'll know the key facts about the Declaration of Independence.

It started off by stating
that we're all created equal.
To make their point, they'd have one chance—
there wouldn't be a sequel.

And so these five men gathered
to write up this declaration,
which told King George,

"Go take a hike! We're
starting a new nation!"

They listed gripes against him and
declared, "We're gone—We're quittin'!
Right now, these 13 colonies
dissolve our ties with Britain!"

In summer 1776,
these words declared our freedom,
when 56 men told the Brits
we didn't really need 'em.

EXTRA CREDIT

The thirteen colonies
officially adopted
the Declaration of
Independence on
July 4, 1776.

WHO WROTE THE DECLARATION OF INDEPENDENCE?

The following five men were asked to draft the Declaration of Independence. Thomas Jefferson did most of the writing.

- Jefferson, Thomas
- Franklin, Benjamin
- Adams, John
- Sherman, Roger
- Livingston, Robert

"Justice For All," Said Leaders!

THE THREE BRANCHES OF THE U.S. GOVERNMENT

Think of the word **jell**. (Yes, *jell* is the root of the word *jelly*!) It means to have two or more things—even people or ideas—take a single form. Jelly is the single form of several ingredients such as fruit, sugar, and something called pectin. When you're trying to remember the THREE branches of the U.S. government, think of the first THREE letters of **JELL** or **JELLY**, and you'll get **J-E-L**:

Judicial

Executive

Legislative

KEY BATTLES OF THE AMERICAN REVOLUTION (1775-1783)

The key battles of the American Revolution were:

The Battle of **Lexington and Concord**
It was fought in 1775 in Massachusetts. (**L** and **C** when said together sound like Elsie, get it?)

The Siege of **Charleston**
It was fought in 1780 in South Carolina.

The Battle of **YOrktown**
It was fought in 1781 in Virginia.

The Battle of **COWPENs**
It was fought in 1781 in South Carolina.

The Battle of **SAratoga**
It was fought in 1777 in New York.

The Battle of **BUNker Hill**
It was fought in 1777 in Massachusetts.

Remember this sentence to memorize these key battles:

ELSIE, Close YOur

COWPEN, SAid BUNny!

THE FIRST 10 PRESIDENTS

The first 10 presidents of the United States are **WASHING**ton, **ADAMS**, **JE**fferson, **MA**dison, **MO**nroe, John Quincy Adams*, **JACK**son, **VA**n Buren, **Harrison****, and **TYLER**.

Note that Madison and Monroe both begin with **M**, so I made my mnemonic word for Madison begin with **MA** and my mnemonic word for Monroe (*MOcked*) begin with **MO**.

* ** See Answer Key on page 44.

Use the following sentence to help you remember presidents one through 10:

1 WASHINGTON	2 ADAMS	3 JEFFERSON	4 MADISON	5 MONROE
1789-1797	1797-1801	1801-1809	1809-1817	1817-1825

WASHING ADAM'S JEans, MA MOcked Aunt JACKie's vAluable Hog, TYLER.

6
J.Q. ADAMS

1825-1829

7
JACKSON

1829-1837

8
VAN BUREN

1837-1841

9
HARRISON

1841-1841

10
TYLER

1841-1845

PRESIDENTS 11 THROUGH 20

Here's a jump rope song to help you remember these next 10 presidents!

That's Polk, Taylor, Fillmore, Pierce, Buchanan, Lincoln, Johnson, Grant, Hayes, and Garfield!

11
POLK
1845-1849

12
TAYLOR
1849-1850

13
FILLMORE
1850-1853

14
PIERCE
1853-1857

15
BUCHANAN
1857-1861

Polk and Taylor, Fillmore, Pierce,
Buchanan, and Abe Lincoln.
Once you memorize these names,
you'll know them without thinkin'.

Johnson, U.S. Grant, and Hayes,
Garfield makes 20.
When it comes to presidents—
I am learning plenty!

16
LINCOLN
1861-1865

17
JOHNSON
1865-1869

18
GRANT
1869-1877

19
HAYES
1877-1881

20
GARFIELD
1881-1881

PRESIDENTS 21 THROUGH 30

The 21st through 30th presidents of the United States are **ARTHUR**, **CLEVE**land, **HA**rrison*, **CLE**veland**, **Mc**Kinley, **RO**osevelt, **TAF**t, **Wilson**, **H**arding, and **COOL**idge.

Memorize this sentence to help you remember them!

* ** See Answer Key on page 44.

ARTHUR CLEVERly HAndles CLEavers, Muffins, Roses, and TAFfy While Hoarding COOLers.

21. ARTHUR	22. CLEVELAND	23. B. HARRISON	24. CLEVELAND	25. McKINLEY
1881-1885	1885-1889	1889-1893	1893-1897	1897-1901

ROOSEVELT
1901-1909

TAFT
1909-1913

WILSON
1913-1921

HARDING
1921-1923

COOLIDGE
1923-1929

PRESIDENTS 31 THROUGH 40

31	32	33	34	35
HOOVER	F. ROOSEVELT	TRUMAN	EISENHOWER	KENNEDY
1929-1933	1933-1945	1945-1953	1953-1961	1961-1963

Hoover's number 31.
Next is **Roosevelt**,
who helped lift the Depression
once his New Deal was dealt.

↓

33 is **Truman**.
Eisenhower's 34.
He got his start at politics
when he returned from war.

↓

35 is **Kennedy**, then
Johnson, Richard Nixon
who got into the kind of mess
for which there was no fixin'.

38 is **Gerald Ford**.
Next is **Jimmy Carter**.
Times were hard when he arrived,
and they got even harder!

↓

Reagan was a film star,
who was handsome,
smooth, and sporty.
These were all our presidents
from 31 to 40!

| 36 JOHNSON | 37 NIXON | 38 FORD | 39 CARTER | 40 REAGAN |
| 1963-1969 | 1969-1974 | 1974-1977 | 1977-1981 | 1981-1989 |

PRESIDENTS 41 THROUGH 44

READ ON!
Get the inside scoop on how Barack Obama became the first African American president in *Barack Obama: President for a New Era* by Marlene Targ Brill.

The 41st through 44th presidents are **George H. W. Bush**, **Bill Clinton, George W. Bush*, and Barack Obama**. Memorize the phrase below and you'll know the first letters of the four presidents' names. Notice also that each word of the mnemonic below has the same number of syllables as the matching president's name.

* See Answer Key on page 44.

For this group of presidents, just remember this simple warning:

Be Careful! Bees Overhead!

BUSH	CLINTON	G.W.BUSH	OBAMA
1989-1993	1993-2001	2001-2009	2009-

THE CONFEDERACY

The 11 states of the Confederacy during the Civil War (1861-1865) were:

MISSissippi, **VIRGINIA**, **LO**uisiana, **NORTH** Carolina, **Alabama**, **SOUTH** Carolina, **Florida**, **Texas**, **TEN**nessee, **AR**kansas, and **Georgia**.

Here is a sentence that will help you memorize the states of the Confederacy:

MISS VIRGINIA LOoked NORTH And SOUTH For The TEN ARmy Guys.

EXTRA CREDIT

During the Civil War, the United States wasn't united at all. Instead, the states in the South became their own country—the Confederacy.

THE UNION

If you can memorize these sentences, the first letter of each word will remind you of one of the 25 Union states during the time of the Civil War.

KAnsas
NEvada
NEW Hampshire
WIsconsin
Delaware★
Ohio
Iowa
Connecticut

KAte's NEat NEWt WIll Dine On Ice Cream.

Kentucky★
Oregon
CAlifornia
WEst Virginia★
Michigan

MEW

Kyle's Old CAt WEnt "Mew."

Vermont
Minnesota
MAssachusetts
Maine
MIssouri★
Maryland★
NEw York

Vick's Mule MAde Me MIghty, Mighty NErvous.

Illinois
Rhode Island
Pennsylvania
Indiana
NEW Jersey

Ike's Red Pig Is NEW.

EXTRA CREDIT

The starred states were on the border with the Confederacy. They were part of the Union, but they also permitted slavery during the Civil War.

THE EMANCIPATION PROCLAMATION

When Lincoln issued the Emancipation Proclamation, he ordered that all the slaves in the Confederacy were free. In what year did he do this? By counting the letters in each of the words in the sentence below, you can remember the year: 1863.

I released slaves now.
1   8   6   3

THE CIVIL WAR ENDS

In what year did the Civil War end? By counting the letters in each of the words in the sentences below, you can remember the year: 1865.

I defeated mighty South.
1   8   6   5

I conclude battle, Grant.
1   8   6   5

EXTRA CREDIT

Confederate general Robert E. Lee surrendered to Union general Ulysses S. Grant at Appomattox Courthouse in Virginia.

U.S. TRAILBLAZERS

Henry Ford introduced the assembly line in 1913. By counting the letters in each of the words in the sentence below, you can remember the year: 1913.

READ ON:
Do you want to know more about
the life of Henry Ford? Check out
Henry Ford by Jeffrey Zuehlke.

In what year did Amelia Earhart become the first woman to fly solo across the Atlantic Ocean? By counting the letters in each of the words in the sentence below, you can remember the year: 1928.

I pioneered U.S. aviation.
1   9   2   8

READ ON:
Read about her famous flights and her mysterious disappearance in *Amelia Earhart* by Jane Sutcliffe.

Sing this song to the tune of "Old MacDonald" to memorize key facts about the first man to orbit Earth: John Glenn.

John Glenn was an as-tro-naut.
Into space he flew.
NASA's first to orbit Earth,
in 1962!

With a liftoff here
and a vroom, vroom there,
on-top-of-an-Atlas-rocket where
John Glenn helped make his-tor-y,
back in '62!

In what year did Neil Armstrong become the first person to walk on the moon? By counting the letters in each of the words in the sentence below, you can remember the year: 1969.

I pioneered Apollo moonwalks.
1 9 6 9

EXTRA CREDIT

The purpose of the Apollo program was to land humans on the moon. Six of the missions achieved this goal. While the astronauts were on the moon's surface, they collected samples and carried out many experiments that significantly added to scientists' knowledge of space.

In what year did Jackie Robinson become the first African American player to enter baseball's major leagues? By counting the letters in each of the words in the sentence below, you can remember the year: 1947.

I shattered race barrier.
1 9 4 7

READ ON!
What do you know about this legendary baseball player? Read *Jackie Robinson* by Stephanie Sammartino McPherson to learn more.

Oh, Sally Ride,
known far and wide,
you earned your Ph.D.
Then NASA had you
orbit Earth in 1983!

Oh, Sally Ride,
you took a ride
that reached beyond the stars:
the first female through space to sail
from this great land of ours!

ANSWER KEY

THE EXPLORATION STATION (pp. 6-13)

Help Tom Scour His Curb. = Christopher Columbus

A Cool Prom = Marco Polo

Treed Hiker = Erik the Red

Far Mainland Legend = Ferdinand Magellan

Acquire Car Jets = Jacques Cartier

Dean, Boil One! = Daniel Boone

Raw Dance Skill = Lewis and Clark

Bulk Pie Zone = Zebulon Pike

THE FIRST 10 PRESIDENTS (pp. 22-23)

* John Quincy Adams was the son of John Adams, the second president.

** William Henry Harrison was the grandfather of future president Benjamin Harrison (see page 26).

PRESIDENTS 21 THROUGH 30 (pp. 26-27)

* Benjamin Harrison was the grandson of William Henry Harrison.

** Grover Cleveland was the 22nd and 24th president. He is the only president to serve two terms with another president in between. After his first term, he lost his reelection bid to Benjamin Harrison. Cleveland was elected again four years later, defeating Harrison.

PRESIDENTS 41 THROUGH 44 (pp. 30-31)

* George W. Bush is the son of George H. W. Bush.

GLOSSARY

American Revolution: the war that America fought with Britain from 1775-1783 to gain independence from British rule (*see* pp. 16-18, 20-21)

Apollo program: a series of U.S. missions into space. The program's goal was to transport astronauts to the moon. (*see* p. 41)

assembly line: an efficient process by which products are put together one piece at a time in a planned order (*see* p. 38)

Bactrian: a two-humped camel (*see* p. 5)

circumnavigate: travel all the way around. To circumnavigate Earth means to go completely around it (*see* p. 9).

Civil War: a war between the Northern and Southern states in 1861-1865 (*see* pp. 32-37)

Confederacy: the states that split from the Union during the Civil War to form their own country where slavery was legal (*see* pp. 32-33)

Declaration of Independence: a document that declared America's freedom from British rule (*see* p. 16-17)

Depression: (1929-1942) a period in history when economies throughout the world were very bad. Many people were extremely poor during this time (*see* p. 29).

dromedary: a one-humped camel (*see* p. 5)

Emancipation Proclamation: an order given by Abraham Lincoln in 1863 that freed the slaves in the Confederate states (*see* p. 36)

executive branch: the president, the vice president, and the cabinet and its agencies. The executive branch is responsible for carrying out laws. (*see* pp. 19, 22-31)

explorer: someone who travels to discover new things (*see* pp. 8-13)

Hispaniola: an island in the Caribbean that contains the countries of Haiti and the Dominican Republic (*see* p. 6)

judicial branch: the Supreme Court, which is made up of nine justices, or judges. The judicial branch interprets laws. (*see* p. 19)

legislative branch: Congress, which is made up of the House of Representatives and the Senate. The legislative branch makes laws. (*see* p. 19)

Louisiana Purchase: the large section of land in the middle of the United States that Thomas Jefferson bought from France in 1803 for $15 million (*see* p. 13)

Mayflower: the ship that brought the pilgrims to the New World (*see* p. 14)

Mayflower Compact: the first agreement about government in the New World. The pilgrims wrote it while on the *Mayflower.* (*see* p. 14-15)

mouth (of a river): the place where a river flows into a larger body of water, like the ocean (*see* p. 10)

NASA: a government-run agency that oversees space exploration and research. It stands for National Aeronautics and Space Administration. (*see* pp. 40, 43)

New Deal: Franklin D. Roosevelt's plan to bring the United States out of the Depression (*see* p. 29)

orbit: to travel in an invisible path around the sun, a star, a planet, or other heavenly body (*see* pp. 40, 43)

pectin: a substance that holds the ingredients in jelly together and makes jelly thick (*see* p. 19)

Silk Road: an ancient trade route between China and the Mediterranean Sea. The Chinese used this route to trade silk for goods from places such as India and Rome. (*see* p. 7)

sources (of rivers): the places where rivers start (*see* p. 13)

Union: the states that stayed loyal and did not join the Confederacy during the Civil War (*see* pp. 34-35)

Vikings: fierce Scandinavian warriors who raided and settled on the coasts of Europe in the 700s to 900s (*see* p. 8)

water route: a way to get from one place to another by traveling on water (*see* p. 12)

READ ON!

BOOKS

Brill, Marlene Targ. *Barack Obama: President for a New Era.* Minneapolis: Lerner Publications Company, 2009.

Brown, Dottie. *Kentucky.* Minneapolis: Lerner Publications Company, 2002.

McPherson, Stephanie Sammartino. *Jackie Robinson.* Minneapolis: Lerner Publications Company, 2010.

Sutcliffe, Jane. *Amelia Earhart.* Minneapolis: Lerner Publications Company, 2003.

Waxman, Laura Hamilton. *Why Did the Pilgrims Come to the New World? And Other Questions about the Plymouth Colony.* Minneapolis: Lerner Publications Company, 2011.

Zuehlke, Jeffrey. *Henry Ford.* Minneapolis: Lerner Publications Company, 2007.

WEBSITES

Ben's Guide to the U.S. Government for Kids
http://bensguide.gpo.gov/
Benjamin Franklin is your personal guide in this tour of the U.S. government, explaining everything from its history to how it functions today.

Kids.gov
http://www.kids.gov/k_5/k_5_social.shtml
Learn more about social studies by following links to facts and articles on government websites.

Presidential Fun Facts
http://www.whitehouse.gov/about/white-house-101/fun-facts
Read fun facts about the past presidents of the United States.

Smithsonian Kids
http://www.smithsonianeducation.org
Visit the Smithsonian's website for kids to find more information about U.S. history. This site includes details about landing on the moon, presidential facts, and fun games to test your knowledge.

Social Studies for Kids
http://www.socialstudiesforkids.com
Follow the links on this site to read about current events and a variety of social studies topics like government, economics, and history.

INDEX

American Revolution, 20-21
Armstrong, Neil, 41

cheerleading leaders, 18
Civil War, 32-37; Confederacy,
 32-33, 36; Union, 34-35

dates, memorizing of, 36-39, 41-42
Declaration of Independence,
 16-18

Earhart, Amelia, 39
Emancipation Proclamation, 36
explorers, 4, 6-8, 9-13, 40-41

Ford, Henry, 38

George (king), 17
Glenn, John, 40

jeans, washing Adam's, 5, 22-23
Jefferson, Thomas, 5, 18, 22

Lincoln, Abraham, 24-25, 36
Louisiana Purchase, 13

Mayflower Compact, 14-15
mnemonics, creating your own,
 4-5

painless tricks for memorizing
 social studies facts, 4-43
poems and rhymes, 16-17, 24-25,
 28-29
presidents, 5, 22-32, 44; one
 through 10, 21-22; 11 through 20,
 24-25; 21 through 30, 26-27; 31
 through 40, 28-29; 41 through
 44, 30-31

rapping, pilgrims, 14
revolutionary cow, escape of,
 20-21
riddles, 6-13
Ride, Sally, 43
Robinson, Jackie, 42

songs, 14-15, 40, 43; jump rope,
 24-25

trailblazers, 38-43

U.S. government, branches of, 19

war, 20-21, 32-37